Mid-Atlantic Network Forest Vegetation Monitoring Protocol

Natural Resource Report NPS/MIDN/NRR—2009/119

James A. Comiskey
Mid-Atlantic Network
National Park Service
120 Chatham Lane
Fredericksburg, VA 22405

John Paul Schmit
National Park Service
Center for Urban Ecology
4598 MacArthur Blvd., NW
Washington DC 2007

and

Geri Tierney
Department of Environmental & Forest Biology
SUNY College of Environmental Science & Forestry
Syracuse, NY 13210

July 2009

U.S. Department of the Interior
National Park Service
Natural Resource Program Center
Fort Collins, Colorado

The National Park Service, Natural Resource Program Center publishes a range of reports that address natural resource topics of interest and applicability to a broad audience in the National Park Service and others in natural resource management, including scientists, conservation and environmental constituencies, and the public.

The Natural Resource Report Series is used to disseminate high-priority, current natural resource management information with managerial application. The series targets a general, diverse audience, and may contain NPS policy considerations or address sensitive issues of management applicability.

All manuscripts in the series receive the appropriate level of peer review to ensure that the information is scientifically credible, technically accurate, appropriately written for the intended audience, and designed and published in a professional manner. This report received formal, high-level peer review based on the importance of its content, or its potentially controversial or precedent-setting nature. Peer review was conducted by highly qualified individuals with subject area technical expertise and was overseen by a peer review manager.

Views, statements, findings, conclusions, recommendations, and data in this report are those of the author(s) and do not necessarily reflect views and policies of the National Park Service, U.S. Department of the Interior. Mention of trade names or commercial products does not constitute endorsement or recommendation for use by the National Park Service.

This report is available from the Mid-Atlantic Network (http://science.nature.nps.gov/im/units/midn/Reports.cfm) and the Natural Resource Publications Management website (http://www.nature.nps.gov/publications/NRPM).

Please cite this publication as:

Comiskey, J. A., J. P. Schmit, and G. Tierney. 2009. Mid-Atlantic Network forest vegetation monitoring protocol. Natural Resource Report NPS/MIDN/NRR—2009/119. National Park Service, Fort Collins, Colorado.

NPS 956/100130, July 2009

Contents

Figures

Tables

Acronyms

APCO: Appomattox Court House National Historical Park

BOWA: Booker T. Washington National Monument

DBH: Diameter at breast height

DOI: U.S. Department of the Interior

EISE: Eisenhower National Historic Site

ERMN: Eastern Rivers and Mountains Network

FGDC: Federal Geographic Data Committee

FHM: Forest Health Monitoring

FIA: Forest Inventory and Analysis Program of USFS

FRSP: Fredericksburg and Spotsylvania National Military Park

GETT: Gettysburg National Military Park

GLKN: Great Lakes Network

GPS: Global Positioning System

GRTS: Generalized Random Tessellation Stratified Design

HOFU: Hopewell Furnace National Historic Site

I&M: Inventory and Monitoring Program

MDC: Minimum Detectable Change

MIDN: Mid-Atlantic Network

NB: National Battlefield

NBP: National Battlefield Park

NCBN: Northeast Coastal and Barrier Network

NCRN: National Capital Region Network

NER: NPS Northeast Region

NETN: Northeast Temperate Network

NHP: National Historical Park

NHS: National Historic Site

NMP: National Military Park

NP: National Park

NPS: National Park Service

NRDT: Natural Resource Database Template

NRPC: Natural Resource Program Center

PETE: Petersburg National Battlefield

RICH: Richmond National Battlefield Park

SHEN: Shenandoah National Park

VAFO: Valley Forge National Historical Park

WASO: Washington-Area Service Office

Executive Summary

The Inventory and Monitoring Program's Mid-Atlantic Network has identified forest vegetation and several associated vital signs as high priority for long-term monitoring. In collaboration with other networks, a protocol has been developed and pilot tested in nine parks of Virginia and Pennsylvania. The forest vegetation monitoring protocol assesses the status and trends of forest plant communities, and the impacts of stressors such as white-tailed deer, invasive exotic plants, exotic plant diseases and pathogens, and native forest pests, as well as the effect of acid deposition on forest soils. Evaluation of snags and downed woody debris provides information on additional important habitat for wildlife. A set of Standard Operating Procedures are shared with the Northeast Temperate Network's forest vegetation monitoring protocol. The current protocol has been designed to sample 300 plots in forested areas of Mid-Atlantic Network and 24 plots in three Northeast Coastal and Barrier Network parks. Plot locations are randomly chosen from a 250-m sampling grid using a spatially balanced design (generalized random-tessellation stratified). Each plot consists of a 20 x 20 m square where all trees and shrubs with a diameter at breast height (dbh) $\geq$ 10 cm are identified, measured, tagged, marked, mapped, and their condition assessed. Trees and shrubs with a dbh $\geq$ 1 cm are identified, measured, marked, and tagged in each of three microplots. Number and height of tree seedlings and cover of a select group of native and invasive herbaceous plants are recorded in twelve quadrats. Coarse woody debris is measured along three transects. Additional metrics will likely be incorporated in future protocol versions including soil sampling and landscape context.

Acknowledgments

We would like to thank members of the National Park Service's Forest Vegetation Working Group who have spent the last three years collaboratively developing the monitoring protocols for networks in the Northeast, National Capital, Midwest, and Southeast Regions. In particular we are indebted to the staff of the National Capital Region Network and Northeast Temperate Network whose protocols form a significant basis for the Mid-Atlantic Network protocol. Our thanks are also extended to Wendy Cass, Shenandoah National Park, for providing a wealth of valuable experience and insights into the development and maintenance of a long term vegetation monitoring program. Kristina Callahan and Sarah Wakamiya have provided invaluable data management and field support, and we are very grateful to our field crews over the last three years including, James Burka, Carolyn Davis, Sophia DeMaio, Erika Gorczyca, Nichole Lightle, Lindsey Sloat, Andrew Vincello, Katherine Wilkin, and Elizabeth Wright. We would also like to thank Elizabeth Johnson, Regional I&M Program Manager, and John Karish, NER Chief Scientist, as well as the park resource managers, including Kristen Allen, Steve Ambrose, Tim Blumenschine, Zachary Bolitho, Brian Eick, Kristina Heister, Gregg Kneipp, Dave Shockley, and Timbo Sims for their continued support for the implementation of all Mid-Atlantic Network inventory and monitoring activities. We are also very grateful to our three reviewers, Mike Jenkins, Will McWilliams, and Chip Scott for their valuable input and feedback. Penelope Pooler provided additional feedback on statistical analyses. Jason Bennett provided guidance and templates for the document layout.

Forest Vegetation Monitoring Protocol

1   Background and Objectives

1.1   Background and History

The forest vegetation monitoring protocol is designed to inventory and monitor forest vegetation in nine parks of the National Park Service (NPS) Mid-Atlantic Network (MIDN) and three parks of the Northeast Coastal and Barrier Network (NCBN) as part of the Inventory and Monitoring Program (I&M). Since 2004, several I&M parks and networks are collaborating to ensure that protocols for tracking forest health allow compatibility with one another and with the United States Forest Service (USFS) Forest Inventory Analysis (FIA) and Forest Health Monitoring (FHM) programs. This protocol is based primarily on protocols developed by the National Capital Region Network (NCRN) (Schmit et al. 2009) and NETN (Northeast Temperate Network) (Tierney et al. 2009), with additional components from Shenandoah National Park (Cass 2007), Great Lakes Network (GLKN) (Sanders et al. 2008) and the Eastern Rivers and Mountains Network (ERMN)(Perles et al. In press). The standard operating procedures (SOPs) are shared with the NETN.

The Mid-Atlantic Network consists of ten parks distributed from southern Pennsylvania to southern Virginia, and extending from the Piedmont to the Coastal Plain (Figure 1). The parks range from the predominantly small, cultural parks with a limited history of natural resource monitoring, to the comparatively large Shenandoah National Park that was designated as one of the prototype monitoring park upon which the I&M vital signs program was developed. All the Mid-Atlantic Network parks are located in eastern deciduous forest that is characterized by pronounced seasons, and strong annual cycles of temperature and precipitation. Richmond National Battlefield Park and the Eastern Front of Petersburg National Battlefield fall within the Coastal Plain which is composed primarily of unconsolidated sand, silt and clay that has been cleared extensively. The Coastal Plain gives way to the Piedmont at the loosely defined fall zone, and it is in this transition zone that Fredericksburg and Spotsylvania National Military Park is located. All other MIDN parks are located within the Piedmont, except for Shenandoah NP that is found exclusively in the Blue Ridge Mountains. Forests of the Blue Ridge vary along altitudinal gradients but are primarily Appalachian Oak Forests. The southern Piedmont and Coastal Plain forests are Southern Mixed forests composed of pines and hardwoods. The Pennsylvania parks are primarily broadleaf forests that form a lowland northerly expression of the Appalachian Oak Forest. In addition, three NCBN parks are included in this monitoring protocol; two are located in the coastal plain (Thomas Stone National Historic Site and George Washington Birthplace National Monument), and the third in the Lower New England ecoregion in Long Island (Sagamore Hill National Historic Site).

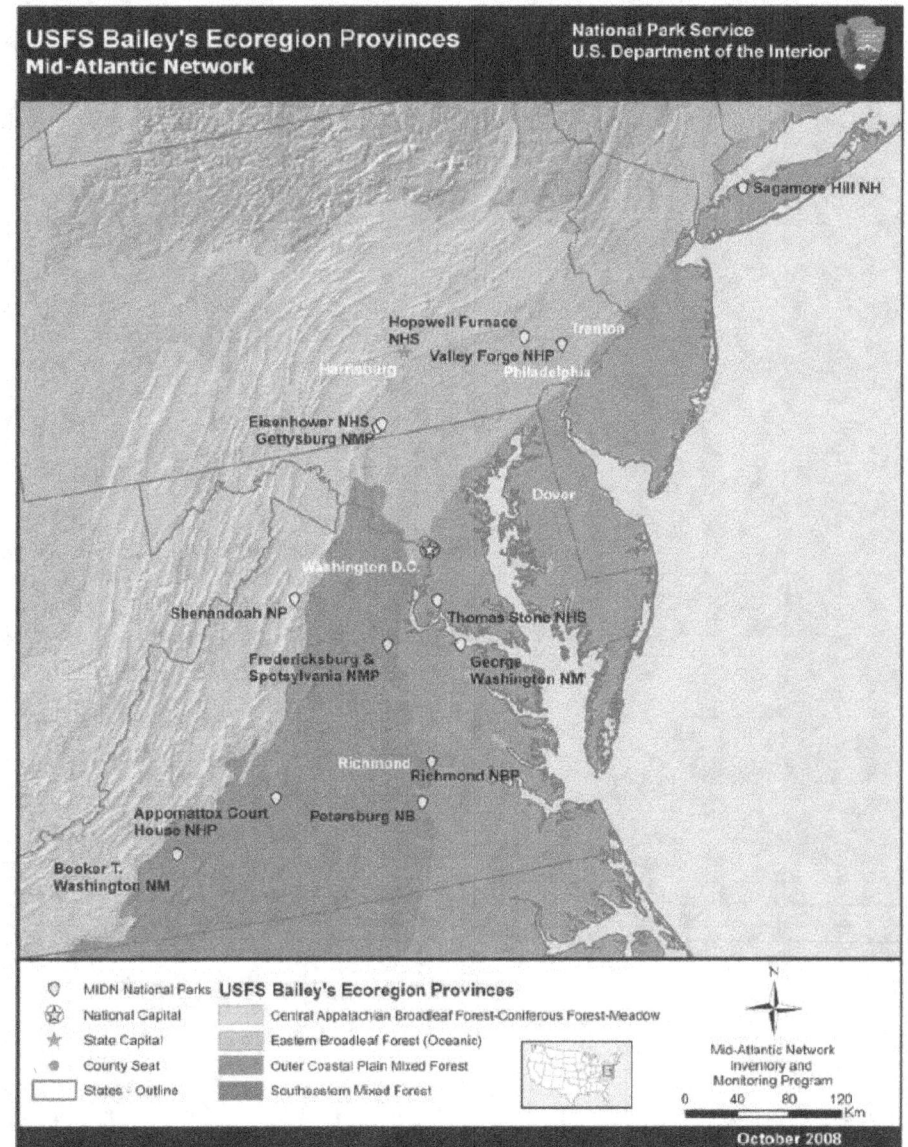

Figure 1. Map of the parks in the Mid-Atlantic Network. Three parks from the Northeast Coastal and Barrier Network are also shown and are included in this monitoring protocol. Shenandoah National Park has its own protocol for monitoring forest vegetation (Cass 2007).

All MIDN have completed vegetation maps with some parks having additional vegetation inventory work. Reports are available for Appomattox Court House National Historical Park (Patterson 2008a), Booker T. Washington National Monument (Patterson 2008b), Fredericksburg and Spotsylvania National Military Park (Taverna and Patterson 2008), Gettysburg National Military Park and Eisenhower National Historic Site (Kunsman 2006, Perles et al. 2006), Hopewell Furnace National Historic Site (Storm et al. 1994, Podniesinski et al. 2005a), Petersburg National Battlefield (Patterson 2008d), Richmond National Battlefield Park (Hayden and Johnson 1986, Hayden et al. 1988, Haskins et al. 1989, Patterson 2008e), and Valley Forge National Historical Park (Podniesinski et al. 2005b). For the NCBN parks, a report has been published for George Washington Birthplace National Monument (Patterson 2008c). Some parks have ongoing monitoring activities led by park staff, for example, historic woodlots at Gettysburg NMP (Bowersox et al. 2002, Larrick et al. 2003, Bowersox et al. 2004, Niewinski et al. 2006), and Valley Forge NHP (Bowersox and Larrick 1999, Diefenbach et al. 2008), while several parks have had vegetation monitoring in the past including Fredericksburg and Spotsylvania NMP (Orwig and Abrams 1994), and Petersburg NB (Rantis and Johnson 1995, 2002).

1.2 Rationale for Monitoring Forest Vegetation

The Mid-Atlantic region is primarily a forested ecoregion and all MIDN parks have forests that form an essential part of the landscape and provide habitat for a diversity of wildlife. For this reason, the vital signs selection process highlighted forest vegetation and several associated indicators as being a high priority for monitoring (Comiskey and Callahan 2008).

The forest vegetation monitoring protocol assesses the status and trends of forest plant communities, and the impacts of stressors such as white-tailed deer, invasive exotic plants, exotic plant diseases and pathogens, and native forest pests, as well as the effect of acid deposition on forest soils. Evaluation of snags and downed woody debris provides information on additional important habitat for wildlife.

Forest structure, composition, and dynamics are important measures of forest condition and health (Yahner 2000). Changes in these metrics can be indicative of stressors that may result in alterations in the future ecological integrity of the forest communities and the species that depend on them (Rutters et al. 1992, Keddy and Drummond 1996). For example, high mortality rates among canopy trees may signal a change in the dominant forest species (Orwig and Abrams 1994, Abrams and Black 2000); declines in seedling and sapling densities could indicate a reduced capacity of the forest to regenerate (McWilliams et al. 2005); or, increases in invasive exotic plant cover could result in the competitive exclusion of other herbaceous plants in the forest understory (Simberloff et al. 2005). Other anthropogenic stressors may have a long-term effect on the forest communities, including acid deposition which can alter soil chemistry, disrupting nutrient cycles (Fowler et al. 1999). Increased habitat fragmentation surrounding parks can weaken the ecological integrity of the forests, increasing their susceptibility to exotic plant and pest invasions (Collinge 1996).

Information from this monitoring protocol will assist parks in managing their natural resources. For example, at Valley Forge National Historical Park in Pennsylvania, deer densities that exceed 200 per square mile have caused a drastic reduction in forest regeneration and the diversity and abundance of herbaceous understory plants. The park hopes to implement deer management efforts, and will use the forest vegetation monitoring data to determine whether future deer densities support healthy regeneration. Likewise, parks where deer densities are on the rise will look to the forest vegetation monitoring data to determine when deer management should be implemented. In addition, information and data will be made available to other agencies and interested parties.

1.3 Measurable Objectives

The overarching goal of the vegetation monitoring program is to provide a framework for monitoring long-term change over broad spatial scales of the Mid-Atlantic Network forests[1]. Specific monitoring objectives include:

1. Determine the status and trends in forest structure, composition, and dynamics of canopy and understory woody species.

2. Determine the status and trends in the density and composition of tree seedlings and selected herbaceous species that are indicators of deer browse.

---

[1] All statements of MIDN in this protocol also include the three NCBN parks.

3. Detect and monitor the presence of invasive exotic plants, exotic plant diseases and pathogens, and forest pests.

4. Determine the status and trends in forest coarse woody debris and the availability of snags.

5. Determine the status and trends in soil Ca:Al and C:N ratios to asses the extent of base cation depletion, increased aluminum availability and/or nitrogen saturation impacting MIDN forest soils.

Inferences will be made on a park, network, and regional basis. For some MIDN parks that are divided into several units, inferences will be made to individual units (Fredericksburg and Spotsylvania NMP and Petersburg NB). The standardized approach will facilitate comparisons across networks and with other agencies (for example, the USFS-FIA Program).

2   Sampling Design

2.1   Sampling Design Rationale

As the first I&M networks initiated protocol development for forest vegetation, an important objective was to have methodologies compatible with approaches used by other agencies and institutions. The Forest Service's FIA Program was seen as a potential model to follow as it has been in use nationwide for over 70 years (McRoberts 2005, USFS 2007). A forest monitoring working group was formed to ensure protocols developed by the networks consisted of standardized metrics and field methods to assure that data sharing is possible. The MIDN actively participated in the working group and has therefore been able to draw heavily from the first networks to develop their protocols, primarily the NETN (Tierney et al. 2009) and the NCRN (Schmit et al. 2009). The resulting protocols, including this one, are based on the FIA approach, but have been modified to meet network objectives and funding constraints.

2.2   Target Population

Forest vegetation monitoring is conducted in all MIDN parks (except Shenandoah NP where a separate protocol is used [Cass 2007]) and three NCBN parks. The target population is restricted to forested areas within each park. Park resource managers actively participated in defining the population to be sampled, with some areas being excluded from the sampling area. For some parks (Fredericksburg and Spotsylvania NMP and Petersburg NB), it

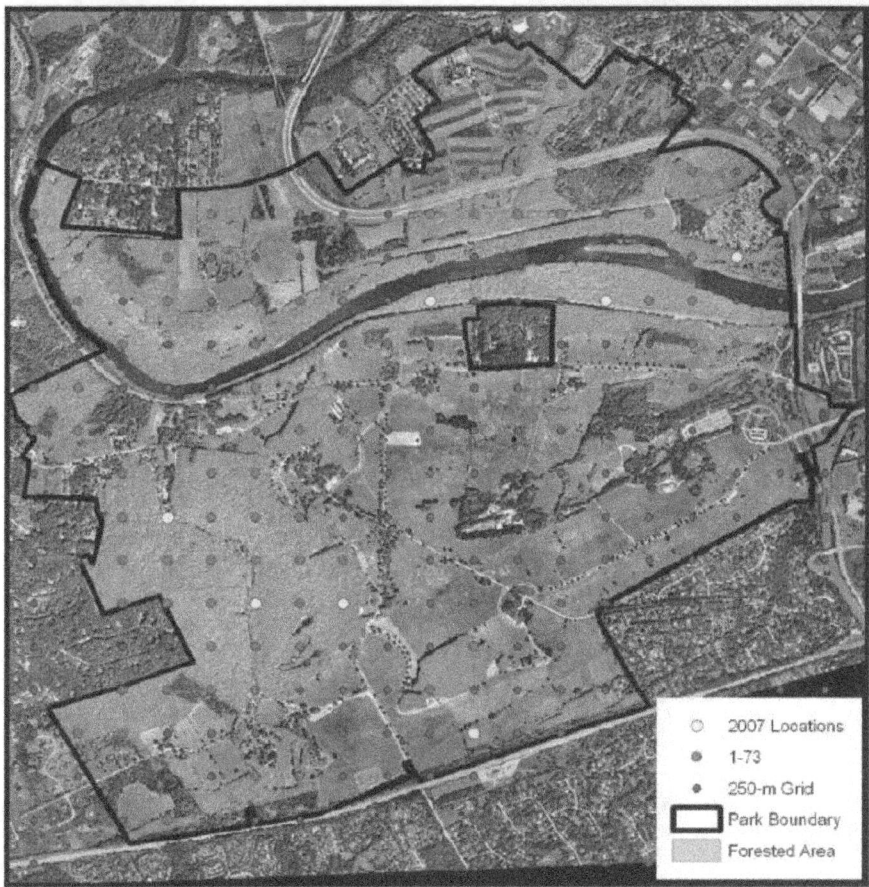

Figure 2. Example of sampling frame at Valley Forge National Historical Park.

was determined that inferences on individual units or groups of units was desirable; for the remaining parks, inferences will be made at a park level.

2.3   Site Selection

Sampling design is based on a 250-m grid developed for the entire network (sampling frame). All points that do not fall within the sampling frame of the target population were discarded. The points within the sampling frame were used as potential sampling locations (Figure 2). Generalized random-tessellation stratified (GRTS), a method that produces a random, spatially balanced sample (Stevens and Olsen 2004), was used to order all potential sampling points for each park or unit. Sampling points are then selected in the order they occur on the list. Sampling locations that do not meet predefined criteria, for example for safety reasons or because the plot was located on a road or trail, can be rejected and the next point on the list selected for sampling. The design provided by GRTS also allows points to be added or subtracted without a loss of spatial balance. Stratification based on vegetation or landscape features has not been incorporated. Stratification by forest type is known to be problematic, as vegetation types change quickly. This complicates analysis and defeats the purpose of the original stratification (Diefenbach and Mahan 2002). An alternative to stratification by vegetation type would be to stratify based on a more permanent feature of the landscape such as slope or aspect but this was rejected. It is not known what responses the current major threats (deer, exotic invasive plants, diseases) would have to these features, which would reduce the benefits of stratification and complicate future analysis. Finally, after the data has been collected it could still be analyzed to determine if changes in forest structure are related to landscape features.

However, inferences on the forest communities at a park, and in some instances by units within a park, are required. Therefore, individual GRTS draws were conducted for the various parks/units, with a minimum number of samples being selected based on the extent of forest (sampled population area).

2.4 Sampling Frequency and Replication

Vegetation monitoring will be conducted each year, but any one plot will only be visited every four years. Yearly plot measurements can cause soil compaction and trampling of the understory which would bias the monitoring data (Urquhart et al. 1998). Additionally, yearly changes in trees and soil are likely to be sufficiently small as to warrant a longer sampling return interval (Urquhart and Kincaid 1999). A four-panel sampling design will be used, where each panel consists of 75 plots in the MIDN and six plots in the NCBN, which will be revisited every fourth year [1-3]. This level of temporal resolution was deemed important for monitoring several of the vital signs in this protocol, namely deer herbivory, invasive exotic plants, native forest pests, and exotic diseases / pathogens – plants. There is no overlap in the panels to evaluate inter-annual changes, but dramatic events (e.g. drought or insect infestations) will be observed for a subset of the plots, events that may be missed if all the plots are visited at the same time every fourth years. Sampling will be conducted between May and October.

2.5 Recommended Number and Location of Sampling Sites

The response design and sample size were determined based on an initial evaluation of data collected by the neighboring National Capital Region Network (NCRN). The MIDN shares many similarities with NCRN in geographic location, park management priorities, and natural resource threats. The MIDN conducted power analysis on data from 100 NCRN plots using various plot and sample sizes (**Appendix A**). We estimated that MIDN would be able to implement a maximum of 300 plots throughout the network given our funding and staffing level. An additional twenty-four plots were included in 2008 for the three NCBN parks. Plots were allocated to each sampling frame based on total forested area (Table 1). Our preliminary analysis of the NCRN data suggest that a minimum of eight plots would be needed to make inferences, and this is confirmed by our own pilot data (see below). Thus, eight plots are the smallest number allocated to any park or unit.

2.6 Level of Change that can be Detected

Preliminary analysis was conducted using data from the first year of pilot testing and implementation (2007). Because no temporal data is available, spatial variability is used as a proxy for variation over time. Temporal variation is likely to be less than that across space, which makes this a conservative estimate of the statistical power of this study(Schmit et al. 2009).

Sample size analysis was used to determine the level of change and sample sizes at a power of 0.8 and an alpha level of 0.1 (Elzinga et al. 1998):

$$MDC = \sqrt{\frac{(s)^2(Z\alpha + Z\beta)^2}{n}}$$

Where, Minimum Detectable Change (MDC) is the smallest level of change that can be detected; s is the standard deviation calculated for all 75 plots; $Z\alpha$ is the z-coefficient using α for the false-change (Type I) error rate of 0.1; $Z\beta$ is the Z-coefficient for the missed-change (Type II) error rate of 0.2 (power 1-β = 0.8); and, n is the number of plots in the sample (75).

$$\% \ Change = \frac{MDC}{mean} \ x \ 100$$

Where % Change (or % effect size) is the percent change that can be detected; and, mean is the average values in the sample (including plots with no values).

Table 1. Allocation of plots at Mid-Atlantic and Northeast Coastal and Barrier Network parks in relation to forested area.

Park	Park unit	Code	Plots	Forested Area (ha)	ha/plot
Mid-Atlantic Network Parks					
Appomattox Court House NHP		APCO	28	442.0	15.8
Booker T. Washington NM		BOWA	8	62.4	7.8
Fredericksburg and Spotsylvania NMP	Fredericksburg	FRSP-F	28	459.6	16.4
	Spotsylvania Court House	FRSP-S	28	430.0	15.4
	Wilderness and Chancellorsville	FRSP-WC	48	1397.9	29.1
Gettysburg NMP		GETT	32	587.7	18.4
Hopewell Furnace NHS		HOFU	16	269.5	16.8
Petersburg NB	Eastern and Western Front	PETE-WE	28	525.3	18.8
	Five Forks	PETE-FF	24	397.4	16.6
Richmond NBP		RICH	32	564.1	17.6
Valley Forge NHP		VAFO	28	427.3	15.3
Northeast Coastal and Barrier Network					
Thomas Stone NHS		THST	8	89.0	11.1
George Washington Birthplace NM		GEWA	8	86.6	10.8
Sagamore Hill NHS		SAHI	8[1]	16.6	2.1
Total			324	5755.6	

[1] It may not be possible to sample eight randomly located plots at SAHI due to the limited area of forest in the park

As a minimum, we want to detect a 50% change after one repeated measure. Because multiple measurements will be taken at each plot, we expect that the power to detect change will increase over time; hence, metrics that have low power in the first recensus could improve as plots are revisited over the years. We assume that data will be analyzed as a paired t-test between the two sampling intervals. In the current analysis, data are multiplied by four to account for the four year design — once all plots have been installed, our sample size will be four times the number of plots than those we used in these initial analyses. In all cases, power analysis is conducted for all plots. For power analysis of species data, plots with no data for a species are included.

2.6.1 Trees

For tree basal area and density at the network level we expect to detect a 6% and 7% change respectively with a power of 0.8 and alpha level of 0.1. A minimum of four plots are needed to detect a 50% change in tree basal area, and six plots for detecting the same level of change in tree density (Table 2). Therefore, in order to make inferences regarding tree populations in a park or unit, we need at least six plots. Because the analysis is based on one quarter of the plots, we are taking a more conservative approach and estimating that we will need a minimum of eight plots, and this is the minimum number allocated to any park or unit.

For individual species across the network, the detectable level of change varies considerably,

Table 2. Level of change in trees based on pilot data collected in 75 Mid-Atlantic Network forest vegetation monitoring plots in 2Table 3. Level of change in saplings and shrubs based on pilot data collected in 75 Mid-Atlantic Network forest vegetation

Species	Plots[1]	Basal area (cm²)				Density			
		Mean[2]	SD[3]	MDC[4]	% Change[5]	Mean[2]	SD[3]	MDC[4]	% Change[5]
Acer rubrum	33	828	2086	300	36%	1.63	2.96	0.43	26%
Carya glabra	12	162	650	94	58%	0.28	0.80	0.11	41%
Carya tomentosa	20	266	687	99	37%	0.55	1.48	0.21	39%
Cornus florida	15	49	131	19	38%	0.36	0.85	0.12	34%
Fagus grandifolia	10	262	1167	168	64%	0.39	1.29	0.19	48%
Ilex opaca	15	97	266	38	40%	0.60	1.66	0.24	40%
Juniperus virginiana	17	85	286	41	48%	0.35	0.83	0.12	34%
Liquidambar styraciflua	31	1190	3311	477	40%	1.92	3.27	0.47	25%
Liriodendron tulipifera	40	2087	4088	588	28%	2.33	5.57	0.80	34%
Nyssa sylvatica	26	619	2044	294	48%	1.51	3.19	0.46	30%
Pinus taeda	15	1399	3513	506	36%	2.93	8.20	1.18	40%
Pinus virginiana	16	797	2449	353	44%	1.53	4.68	0.67	44%
Prunus serotina	9	50	162	23	47%	0.16	0.47	0.07	42%
Quercus alba	40	1911	3019	435	23%	2.35	3.81	0.55	23%
Quercus coccinea	12	257	951	137	53%	0.29	0.87	0.12	43%
Quercus falcata	9	88	290	42	47%	0.16	0.49	0.07	44%
Quercus rubra	31	744	1573	226	30%	0.88	1.68	0.24	27%
Quercus velutina	20	455	1094	157	35%	0.59	1.32	0.19	32%
Total	75	13295	5103	734	6%	22.56	10.37	1.492	7%

[1] Number of plots that a species occurs in

[2] Mean basal area or density calculated for all 75 plots

[3] Standard deviation of the basal area or density calculated for all 75 plots

[4] Minimum Detectable Change, the smallest level of change that can be detected at $\alpha = 0.1$ and Power $(1-\beta) = 0.8$

[5] MDC expressed as a percentage of the mean

with only 18 of the most common species allowing us to detect at least a 50% change in basal area or density given our current sample sizes (Table 2). Where the detectable level of change is above 50%, the primary cause is that species occur in only a few plots or there is high variability in density or basal area across plots. As more plots are added to our sample, there will be a likely reduction in the variability, as will sampling the same plots over time.

2.6.2 Saplings and shrubs

A challenge in sampling multiple metrics in the same plots is that power to detect change will likely vary depending on what is being measured. In the case of saplings and shrubs, the power to detect change was generally lower than with trees, primarily due to the lower number of individuals measured. Our pilot data indicated that we would be able to detect a 12% change in the basal area and 14% change in density of saplings and shrubs (Table 3). With this estimated level of change, we will need at

least 18 plots to detect a 50% change in basal area, and 24 plots to detect the same change in tree density.

As was seen with the tree data, for most individual species of saplings and shrubs across the network, our power to detect change was low. Only for the most common understory species was is it possible to detect a 50% change in density or basal area (Table 3). Addition of plots in the next few years will provide better estimates.

2.6.3 Seedling regeneration

Forest regeneration is seriously impacted by deer grazing in some of the network parks. We will be evaluating stocking rate using metrics developed by McWilliams (2005) for Pennsylvania. Tree seedlings are assigned a score based on their height class. Healthy stocking rates are achieved when an average of two seedling scores are registered per 1 m². We conducted a sample size analysis on our pilot data and found that on average there were 5.1 seedlings / m² across the network, and we would be able to monitoring plots in 2007.

Species	Plots[1]	Basal area (cm²)				Density			
		Mean[2]	SD[3]	MDC[4]	% Change[5]	Mean[2]	SD[3]	MDC[4]	% Change[5]
Acer rubrum	31	20.1	39.4	5.7	28%	1.23	2.25	0.32	26%
Carpinus caroliniana	12	12.0	46.9	6.8	56%	0.75	2.45	0.35	47%
Carya tomentosa	9	2.1	7.6	1.1	52%	0.25	0.82	0.12	47%
Cornus florida	24	22.6	47.4	6.8	30%	1.44	3.37	0.49	34%
Fraxinus americana	9	2.7	17.6	2.5	93%	0.17	0.58	0.08	48%
Ilex opaca	27	14.4	35.8	5.2	36%	0.99	1.72	0.25	25%
Liquidambar styraciflua	18	12.5	36.1	5.2	42%	0.59	1.51	0.22	37%
Nyssa sylvatica	29	18.2	40.0	5.8	32%	1.28	2.17	0.31	24%
Quercus alba	21	19.9	56.5	8.1	41%	0.89	2.28	0.33	37%
Quercus velutina	9	5.8	30.1	4.3	75%	0.24	0.79	0.11	47%
Sassafras albidum	8	4.4	17.3	2.5	56%	0.17	0.58	0.08	48%
Total	75	227.3	193.1	27.8	12%	14.59	14.31	2.06	14%

[1] Number of plots that a species occurs in

[2] Mean basal area or density calculated for all 75 plots

[3] Standard deviation of the basal area or density calculated for all 75 plots

[4] Minimum Detectable Change, the smallest level of change that can be detected at $\alpha = 0.1$ and Power $(1-\beta) = 0.8$

[5] MDC expressed as a percentage of the mean

detect 10.4% change in the seedling score with a power of 0.8 and alpha level of 0.1. At the individual park level, such as at Gettysburg NMP, our detectable level of change is 21.4%, while at Valley Forge NHP the rate is 57.8%.

3 Field Methods

Detailed methods and field procedures are outlined in the Standard Operating Procedures (SOPs) for the protocol. These SOPs are maintained and shared with the NETN. Table 4 provides a summary of SOPs their content.

3.1 Safety

The Northeast Temperate Network (NETN) and the Mid-Atlantic Network (MIDN) consider the occupational health and safety of their employees, cooperators, and volunteers to be of utmost importance, and are committed to ensuring that all seasonal field technicians receive adequate training on National Park Service (NPS) safety procedures, incident reporting, and emergency response prior to field work. Emergency procedures and contacts, incident reporting, field preparation, safe field procedures, vehicle safety, and workers compensation procedures are outlined in SOP 1 (Safety procedures).

3.2 Field Season Preparations and Equipment Setup

Prior to the field season, all equipment should be reviewed against the equipment list, and tested to ensure proper functioning. Any consumable items (tags, nails, paint etc.) should be ordered if sufficient quantities are not in stock. Plot markers should be stamped and affixed to rebar. Necessary permits should be obtained and park housing reserved. Maps of plot locations are prepared and sample points uploaded to the GPS. Additional details and a full list of equipment is provided in SOP 2 (Preparation and equipment list).

3.3 Field Season Scheduling

Field work is conducted between May and October. In 2008, the MIDN tested a combined field team approach with the NETN. The field crew, consisting of two teams working independently, conducted field work in the NETN parks between May and July, with August to October dedicated to the MIDN parks.

3.4 Technician Training

A one-week training session is conducted each year at the beginning of the field season. Training for the combined MIDN/NETN field team took place at Acadia National Park in 2008 and at Valley Forge National Historical Park in 2009.

Table 4. List of Standard Operating Procedures shared between the MIDN and the NETN. SOPs are available in Tierney et al. (2009). One NCRN SOP is also referenced in this table and is available in Schmit et al. (2009).

SOP # and title	SOP #
Safety procedures	1
Preparation and equipment list	2
Using the Global Positioning System –Garmin 60CSX	3
Using the Laser Rangefinder (LAR)	4
Data management and quality assurance/quality control	5
Site selection and plot establishment	6
Photopoint	7
Stand and site measurements	8
Tree measurements	9
Unknown plant collection	NCRN SOP 11
Microplot measurements	10
Coarse woody debris	11
Soil measurements and sampling	12
Quadrat measurements	13
Landscape context	14
Analyzing and reporting ecological integrity	15
Deviations, differences, and summary of major changes	16

A training manual is currently under development and will be included as an additional SOP. In addition, the project leads spend a second week, subsequent to the training, with the field crew as they implement the protocol, and again sporadically throughout the season. The field crew are instructed to address any questions and uncertainties while still at the plot — each team has at least one cell phone available.

3.5 Details of Taking Measurements, and Post-Collection Processing

3.5.1 Plot location

Field teams navigate to the plot locations that have previously been uploaded to the GPS (SOP 3: Using the Global Positioning System –Garmin 60CSX). Sampling locations that do not meet predefined criteria (Table 5), for example are not forested or fall on a road or

Table 5. Criteria for rejecting plot locations

Category	Criteria
Safety	>30° slope
	Hazardous access
Biological	<25% forest cover in an area not designated for forest regeneration, e.g. early successional stand
	Any portion of the plot overlaps a large trail, road, or river. Small trails and streams that pass through the plot are acceptable
Cultural	Establishment would disturb sensitive cultural resources, e.g. earthworks

trail, are rejected and the next point on the list selected for sampling. A GPS measurement is recorded for the plot center using a minimum of 100 averaged points (SOP 3).

3.5.2 Plot establishment

Once the site has been verified, the plot is established using the procedures outlined in SOP 6 (Site selection and plot establishment). The plot consists of a 20 m x 20 m square with three nested microplots and 12 quadrats (Figure 3). A laser rangefinder is used to establish the plot boundaries (SOP 4: Using the Laser Rangefinder). PVC posts are used to mark the plot corners and the microplots; a survey marker attached to rebar is placed at the plot center.

3.5.3 Stand and site measurements

Information is recorded that describes the site, including, slope, aspect, physiographic class, stand structure and height, crown closure, ground cover and disturbance, microtopography, and presence of water (SOP 8: Stand and site measurements).

3.5.4 Plot photopoints

A series of digital photographs are taken from the plot center (SOP 7: Photopoint). The camera date and time feature is verified to ensure the resulting file will have the correct date stamp.

3.5.5 Field measurements

All trees and shrubs with a diameter at breast height (dbh) ≥ 10 cm in the main plot are identified, measured, tagged, marked, their location mapped using the laser rangefinder, and their condition assessed (SOP 9: Tree measurements). Trees and shrubs with a dbh ≥ 1 cm are identified, measured, marked, and tagged in each of the three microplots (SOP 10: Microplot measurements). Number and height of tree seedlings and cover of a select group of native and invasive herbaceous plants are measured in the quadrats (SOP 13: Quadrat measurements). Coarse woody debris is measured along the transects (SOP 11: Coarse woody debris). Any plant species that cannot be identified in the field are collected (NCRN SOP 11: Unknown plant collection).

Additional field measurements will be added in the future including those currently in use by the NETN such as soil sampling (SOP 12: Soil measurements and sampling), landscape context (SOP 14: Landscape context). Differences between the networks and major changes

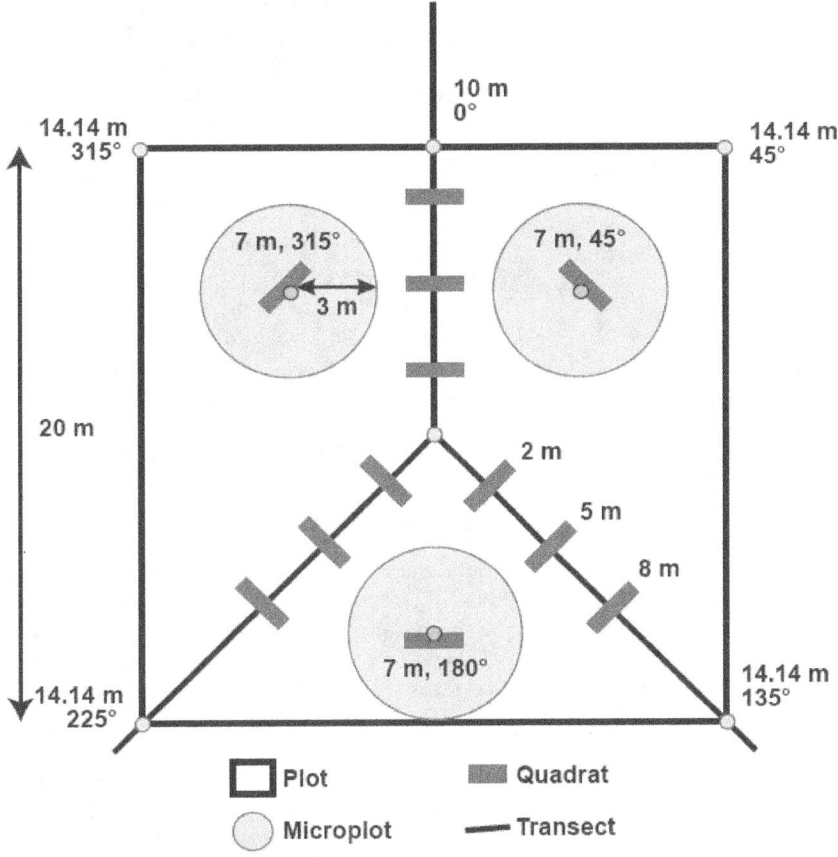

Plot **Quadrat** **Microplot** **Transect**

to SOPs are documented (SOP 16: Deviations, differences, and summary of major changes). Any new measurements will be documented as SOPs.

3.6 QA/QC

Approximately 5% of sampled plots will be resampled annually to determine reliability of data collection. Additional methods for quality control and quality assurance are specified within Data management and QA/QC (SOP 5).

4 Data Handling, Analysis, and Reporting

4.1 Metadata Procedures

Data compiled by the MIDN must be accompanied by FGDC compliant metadata. This includes both spatial and non-spatial datasets. Specific metadata requirements are outlined in the NER Biological Metadata Tools SOP.

4.2 Overview of Database Design

The project database is based on the back-end database design of the Natural Resources Database Template (NRDT). The original database

Figure 3. Layout of Mid-Atlantic Network forest vegetation monitoring plot consisting of one 20 x 20 m plot, three 3-m diameter microplots, 12 2 m x 0.5 m quadrats, and three 15-m transects.

was developed by the ERMN and is currently being adapted as a combined MIDN/NETN database. The database incorporates many functions and utilities to help reduce the possibility of data entry errors and promote data integrity.

4.3 Data Entry, Verification, and Editing

Our original intent was to enter data in the field using a tablet PC. Given the range of measurements and the small team size (2 people), data entry in the field was not practical and risked jeopardizing the quality of the measurements collected. Therefore, during the first four years of plot establishment, data is being entered on field datasheets and transferred to the database once a week. Once recensus of plots is initiated, field computers running the Access database will be used to record information. At that time, the crew will not be installing new plots and therefore the team has fewer tasks and more time to record data in a field computer. This will reduce data entry errors and provide additional quality control in the field.

4.4 Data Analysis

The MIDN will follow the ecological integrity metrics developed by the NETN, which includes calculation of a range of forest metrics (SOP 15: Analyzing and reporting ecological integrity). As outlined in the NETN forest monitoring protocol (Tierney et al. 2009), the MIDN will estimate status and trends over time of specific measures in forested systems of each sampled park. Analyses will be based on a general linear model which partitions spatial and temporal variability to allow assessment of change over time, as is done by the USFS FIA program (Woodall and Monleon 2008).

4.5 Data Archival Procedures

Where data is collected on field forms, these will be scanned and stored in electronic format. Data entered into computers, either in the field or in the office, will be backed up on a daily basis to an external hard drive which will be uploaded to the MIDN server weekly. Long term archival is conducted through a cooperative agreement with North Carolina State University.

4.6 Reporting Schedule and Format

The MIDN will produce annual data summary reports on each year's field work and results of the ecological integrity metrics. Upon completion of each panel (every four years), a more detailed report will provide information on the status and trends in forest metrics at each of the parks and the network as whole. Ad-hoc reports and scientific papers will be published as appropriate.

5 Personnel Requirements and Training

5.1 Roles, Responsibilities, and Qualifications

This forest monitoring protocol is implemented by a crew leader and technician in addition to contract botanists as needed. If two teams are hired, the crew leader will alternate working with each team.

5.1.1 Vegetation Ecologist (Network Coordinator)

The Vegetation Ecologist operates as the project manager to oversee the implementation of the monitoring program including:

- Permits, scheduling, hiring, purchasing, and contracting

- Maintain and update forest vegetation monitoring protocol

- Conduct training and participate in field work as needed

- Oversee field crew, providing logistical, administrative, and technical support

- Ensure QA/QC standards are met

- Analyze data and prepare reports

5.1.2 Data Manager

The MIDN Data Manager provides oversight for all data related aspects of the project including:

- Provide database training to crew

- Maintain forest monitoring database

- Prepare maps of sample point locations

- Ensure data management practices are met, including data backup, transfer, and archiving

- Conduct training and participate in field work as needed

5.1.3 Vegetation Crew Leader

The Crew Leader is responsible for managing the vegetation crew and must have a strong knowledge of the flora of the mid-Atlantic region. Tasks include:

- Coordinate daily field activities and ensure equipment is in working order

- Coordinate directly with park resource managers when conducting field work

- Ensure that all field crew members are following proper data collection procedures

- Identify plants accurately and/or process unknown plants for later identification

- Conduct data verification if data from paper field sheets were entered into database

- Ensure that all data undergoes the proper QA/QC procedures

- Maintain crew time sheets

5.1.4 Vegetation Crew Technicians

The Crew Technicians are responsible for data collection and must have a working knowledge of the flora of the mid-Atlantic region. Tasks include:

- Collect field data accurately as described in the SOPs

- Identify plants accurately and/or process unknown plants for later identification

- Enter data accurately into the project database either in the field or from paper data sheets

- Ensure all necessary equipment is assembled, clean and functional prior to each trip

5.1.5 Botanist

A botanist will be contracted as needed to either work with the teams during the training session or to revisit plots established by the crews to verify identifications. The Botanist should have an expert knowledge of the mid-Atlantic region flora.

5.2 Training Procedures

A one-week training session is conducted in mid-May to review SOPs and practice establishment of forest monitoring plots (SOP 1: Preparation and equipment). Training should address health and safety concerns and emergency procedures. We also recommend that the network ecologist or data manager work with the field crew during the first full week following training.

Category	Expense ($)
Seasonal staff	25,000
Travel	10,000
Vehicle	4,000
Equipment	5,000
Supplies	1,000
Total	45,000

6 Operational Requirements

6.1 Annual Workload and Field Schedule

Field work is conducted between mid-May and the end of September. If the field crew is hired with the NETN where two teams (crew leader and three technicians) implement the field work, then the first half of the season (mid-May to the end of July) will be spent in NETN parks, and the remaining two months is spent in the MIDN parks.

6.2 Facility and Equipment Needs

The field crew is based at Fredericksburg and Spotsylvania NMP in Virginia. Whenever possible while traveling to the parks, the crew will stay in park housing. Where park housing is not available, the field crew will stay at hotels. All equipment needed to conduct the field work is in listed in SOP 1 (Preparation and equipment list). The crew leader is responsible for ensuring that all equipment is in working order and coordinating with the network staff to replenish supplies as needed.

6.3 Startup Costs and Budget Considerations

The startup costs are based on the costs associated with plot establishment in 2008. Costs include personnel, supplies, and travel. Additional costs will be incurred to replace or repair equipment including computers, GPS units, cameras, and the Laser Ace Rangefinder. These equipment costs are estimated over a five year replacement cycle.

Table 6. Annual budget for implementing the MIDN Forest Vegetation Monitoring Protocol. Figures are based on expenses incurred during the 2008 field season.

007.

7 Literature Cited

Abrams, M. D. and B. A. Black. 2000. Dendroecological analysis of a mature loblolly pine-mixed hardwood forest at the George Washington Birthplace National Monument, eastern Virginia. Journal of the Torrey Botanical Society 127(2):139-148.

Bowersox, T. W. and D. S. Larrick. 1999. Long-term vegetation monitoring of forested ecosystems at Hopewell Furnace National Historic Site and Valley Forge National Historical Park. Technical Report NPS/PHSO/NRTR— 99/077, National Park Service, PHSO, Philadelphia, PA.

Bowersox, T. W., D. S. Larrick, A. T. Niewinski, G. L. Storm, and W. M. Tzilkowski. 2004. Long Term Monitoring of Woodlot Plant Communities at Gettysburg National Military Park. Technical Report NPS/NERCHAL/NRTR— 04/092, National Park Service. Northeast Region, Philadelphia, PA.

Bowersox, T. W., D. S. Larrick, G. L. Storm, and W. M. Tzilkowski. 2002. Regenerating mixed-oak historic woodlots at Gettysburg National Military Park. pages NPS/PHSO/NRTR— 02/086, National Park Service. Mid-Atlantic Regional Office, Philadelphia, PA.

Cass, W. 2007. Shenandoah National Park Long-Term Ecological Monitoring System Forest Monitoring Component. Shenandoah National Park, National Park Service, Luray, VA.

Collinge, S. 1996. Ecological consequences of habitat fragmentation: Implications for landscape architecture and planning. Landscape and Urban Planning 36(1):59-77.

Comiskey, J. A. and K. K. Callahan. 2008. Mid-Atlantic Network vital signs monitoring plan. Natural Resource Report NPS/MIDN/NRR— 2008/071, National Park Service, Fort Collins, CO.

Diefenbach, D., W. Vreeland, and K. M. Heister. 2008. Statistical Analysis of Understory Vegetation Data from Valley Forge National Historical Park, Pennsylvania, 1993-2003. Technical Report NPS/NER/NRTR—2008/118, National Park Service, Philadelphia, PA.

Diefenbach, D. R. and C. Mahan. 2002. Setting realistic objectives: Vegetation inventory and monitoring at Shenandoah National Park. Technical Report NPS/PHSO/NRTR—02/087, National Park Service, Philadelphia, PA.

Elzinga, C. L., D. W. Salzer, and J. H. Willoughby, editors. 1998. Measuring and monitoring plant populations. Bureau of Land Management, Denver, CO.

Fowler, D., J. N. Cape, M. Coyle, C. Flechard, J. Kuylenstierna, K. Hicks, D. Derwent, C. Johnson, and D. Stevenson. 1999. The global exposure of forests to air pollutants. Water Air and Soil Pollution 116(1-2):5-32.

Haskins, M., M. Johnson, and J. Gardner. 1989. Flora of Richmond National Battlefield Park Virginia USA. Castanea 54(2):87.

Hayden, W. J., M. L. Haskins, and M. F. Johnson. 1988. Flora of Richmond National Battlefield Park (Beaver Dam Creek, Malvern Hill, and Parker's Battery units). MAR-27, National Park Service. Mid-Atlantic Regional Office, Philadelphia, PA.

Hayden, W. J. and M. F. Johnson. 1986. Flora of Richmond National Battlefield Park (Chickahominy Bluffs, Cold Harbor, Fort Darling, Fort Harrison, Garthright House, and Watt House Units). MAR-16, National Park Service. Mid-Atlantic Regional Office, Philadelphia, PA.

Keddy, P. A. and C. G. Drummond. 1996. Ecological properties for the evaluation, management, and restoration of temperate deciduous forest ecosystems. Ecological Applications 6(3):748-762.

Kunsman, J. 2006. Inventory of plant species of special concern at Gettysburg National Military Park and Eisenhower National Historic Site. Technical Report NPS/NER/NRTR—2006/042, National Park Service, Philadelphia, PA.

Larrick, D. S., T. W. Bowersox, G. L. Storm, and W. M. Tzilkowski. 2003. Artificial Oak Regeneration in Historic Woodlots at Gettysburg National Military Park. Northern Journal of Applied Forestry 20(3):131-136.

McRoberts, R. E. 2005. The enhanced forest inventory and analysis program. in W. A. Bechtold and P. L. Patterson, editors. The enhanced forest inventory and analysis program - national sampling design and estimation procedures. Gen. Tech. Rep. SRS-80. U.S. Department of Agriculture, Forest Service, Southern Research Station, Asheville, NC.

McWilliams, W. H., T. W. Bowersox, P. H. Brose, D. A. Devlin, J. C. Finley, K. W. Gottschalk, S. Horsley, S. L. King, B. M. LaPoint, T. W. Lister, L. H. McCormick, G. W. Miller, C. T. Scott, H. Steele, K. C. Steiner, S. L. Stout, J. A. Westfall, and R. L. White 2005. Measuring tree seedlings and associated understory vegetation in

Pennsylvania's forests. Pages 21-26 *in* Proceedings of the fourth annual forest inventory and analysis symposium. Gen. Tech. Rep. NC-252. U.S. Department of Agriculture, Forest Service, North Central Research Station, St. Paul, MN.

Niewinski, A. T., T. W. Bowersox, and R. L. Laughlin. 2006. Vegetation Status in Selected Woodlots at Gettysburg National Military Park Pre and Post White-tailed Deer Management. pages Technical Report NPS/NER/NRTR— 2006/037, National Park Service, Philadelphia, PA.

Orwig, D. A. and M. D. Abrams. 1994. Land-use history (1720-1992), composition, and dynamics of oak-pine forests within the Piedmont and Coastal Plain of northern Virginia. Canadian Journal of Forest Research **24**:1216-1225.

Patterson, K. D. 2008a. Vegetation Classification and Mapping at Appomattox Court House National Historical Park, Virginia. Technical Report NPS/NER/NRTR—2008/125, National Park Service, Philadelphia, PA.

Patterson, K. D. 2008b. Vegetation Classification and Mapping at Booker T. Washington National Monument, Virginia. Technical Report NPS/NER/NRTR—2008/100, National Park Service, Philadelphia, PA.

Patterson, K. D. 2008c. Vegetation Classification and Mapping at George Washington Birthplace National Monument, Virginia. Technical Report NPS/NER/NRTR—2008/099, National Park Service, Philadelphia, PA.

Patterson, K. D. 2008d. Vegetation Classification and Mapping at Petersburg National Battlefield. Technical Report NPS/NER/NRTR—2008/127, National Park Service, Philadelphia, PA.

Patterson, K. D. 2008e. Vegetation Classification and Mapping at Richmond National Battlefield Park, Virginia. Technical Report NPS/NER/NRTR—2008/128, National Park Service, Philadelphia, PA.

Perles, S. J., J. Finley, and M. R. Marshall. In press. Vegetation monitoring protocol for the Eastern Rivers and Mountains Network, Version 1.0. Natural Resource Report NPS/ERMN/NRR—2009/xxx, National Park Service, Fort Collins, CO.

Perles, S. J., G. S. Podniesinski, W. A. Millinor, and L. A. Sneddon. 2006. Vegetation Classification and Mapping at Gettysburg National Military Park and Eisenhower National Historic Site. Technical Report NPS/NER/NRTR—2006/058, National Park Service, Philadelphia, PA.

Podniesinski, G. S., S. J. Perles, L. A. Sneddon, and B. Millinor. 2005a. Vegetation Classification and Mapping of Hopewell Furnace National Historic Site. Technical Report NPS/NER/NRTR—2005/012, National Park Service, Philadelphia, PA.

Podniesinski, G. S., L. A. Sneddon, J. Lundgren, H. Devine, B. Slocumb, and F. Koch. 2005b. Vegetation Classification and Mapping of Valley Forge National Historical Park. Technical Report NPS/NER/NRTR—2005/028, National Park Service, Philadelphia, PA.

Rantis, P. A. and J. E. Johnson. 1995. Forest management and the restoration of historic scenes. Technical report NPS/MARPPNBP/NRTR—95, National Park Service, Philadelphia, PA.

Rantis, P. A. and J. E. Johnson. 2002. Understory development in canopy gaps of pine and pine-hardwood forests of the upper Coastal Plain of Virginia. Plant Ecology **159**(1):103-115.

Rutters, K. H., B. E. Law, R. C. Kucera, A. L. Gallant, R. L. DeVelice, and C. J. Palmer. 1992. A selection of forest condition indicators for monitoring. Environmental Monitoring and Assessment **20**(1):21-33.

Sanders, S., S. E. Johnson, and D. M. Waller. 2008. Vegetation monitoring protocol: Great Lakes Inventory & Monitoring Network. Natural Resource Report NPS/GLKN/NRR—2008/056, National Park Service, Fort Collins, CO.

Schmit, J. P., G. Sanders, M. Lehman, and T. Paradis. 2009. National Capital Region Network long-term forest monitoring protocol. Natural Resource Report NPS/NCRN/NRR—2009/113, National Park Service, Fort Collins, CO.

Simberloff, D., I. Parker, and P. Windle. 2005. Introduced species policy, management, and future research needs. Frontiers in Ecology and the Environment **3**(1):12-20.

Stevens, D. L. and A. R. Olsen. 2004. Spatially Balanced Sampling of Natural Resources. Journal of the American Statistical Association **99**(465):262.

Storm, G. L., W. M. Tzilkowoski, T. W. Bowersox, and S. E. Fairweather. 1994. Plant community development in historic forest stands at Hopewell Furnace National Historic Site. NPS/MARHOFU/NRTR— 94/062, National Park Service. Mid-Atlantic Regional Office, Philadelphia, PA.

Taverna, K. and K. D. Patterson. 2008. Vegetation Classification and Mapping at Fredericksburg and Spotsylvania National Military Park. Technical Report NPS/NER/NRTR—2008/126, National Park Service, Philadelphia, PA.

Tierney, G., B. Mitchell, K. Miller, J. Comiskey, A. Kozlowski, and D. Faber-Langendoen. 2009. Long-term forest monitoring protocol and SOPs for the Northeast Temperate Network. Natural Resources Report NPS/NETN/NRR—2009/117, National Park Service, Fort Collins, CO.

Urquhart, N. S. and T. M. Kincaid. 1999. Designs for Detecting Trend from Repeated Surveys of Ecological Resources. Journal of Agricultural, Biological, and Environmental Statistics 4(4):404-414.

Urquhart, N. S., S. G. Paulsen, and D. P. Larsen. 1998. Monitoring for policy-relevant regional trends over time. Ecological Applications 8(2):246-257.

USFS. 2007. Tracking our Nation's vital forest resources. Science Update SRS-011, U.S. Department of Agriculture, Forest Service, Southern Research Station, Asheville, NC.

Woodall, C. and V. Monleon. 2008. Sampling protocols, estimation, and analysis procedures for the down woody materials indicator of the FIA program. General Technical Report NRS-22, USDA Forest Service, Northern Research Station.

Yahner, R. H., editor. 2000. Eastern deciduous forest: Ecology and wildlife conservation. 2nd ed edition. University of Minnesota Press, Minneapolis, MN.

Appendix A

An evaluation of National Capital Region Network
data to assist in developing the
Mid-Atlantic Network sampling strategy

James A. Comiskey

Ecologist, Mid-Atlantic Network

1.1 Introduction

In developing the Mid-Atlantic Network (MIDN) Forest Monitoring Protocol, our first step was to determine the optimal number and size of plots given the limited resources available to the network. In particular, we realized that in order to establish plots in all network parks and be able to make inferences regarding the vegetation communities in each park would require a large number of plots – at least 300 plots throughout the network. Thus in order to increase our number of sample plots we would likely need to sacrifice the size of each plot. Our major concern was whether smaller plots would allow us to detect meaningful levels of change among trees $\geq$ 10 cm in diameter (DBH).

The National Capital Region Network (NCRN) had completed one year of implementation (Schmit and Campbell 2007). Like the MIDN, many of the NCRN parks are small, cultural landscapes located in rapidly urbanizing environments of the Coastal Plain and Piedmont. National Capital Region Network staff provided MIDN with data from 100 forest plots. All trees with a DBH $\geq$ 10 cm in a 15-m radius circle were identified, measured, mapped, and tagged.

1.2 Objective

For the pilot data analysis, MIDN wanted to evaluate how varying the number and size of plots affected the level of power to detect change. Our objectives were to:

- Determine the optimal plot size

- Determine the number of plots

1.3 Methods

We used NCRN data collected in 2006 as part of the Forest Monitoring program's first year of sampling (Schmit and Campbell 2007). Our major assumption was that the forest composition and structure in NCRN would be similar to that found in MIDN parks. The NCRN plots are circular with a 15-m radius (707 m²). MIDN was considering using 20 x 20 m square plots (400 m²) – 57% smaller area. In addition, NCRN would be implementing a total of 400 plots over four years, while MIDN was considering implementing only 300 plots over four years.

The questions addressed

- What is the potential decline in the effect size or minimum detectable change (MDC) for smaller plots compared to the NCRN circles?

- How does the MDC vary depending on the final number of plots established by MIDN?

- How does MDC vary for tree density and basal area for the network and individual parks?

- What species are lost from the study when smaller plots are used?

Because the trees in the 15-m circular plots were mapped, it was possible to isolate and analyze the data of those trees that occurred in a virtual 20 x 20 m area. Power curves were generated to determine the percent detectable change at different power levels with an alpha (α) level of 0.1, for each of the following total sample sizes:

- 400 NCRN plots (15-m circular)

- 400 square plots (20 x 20 m) – x 1 the number of NCRN plots

- 300 square plots (20 x 20 m) – x 0.75 the number of NCRN plots

- 200 square plots (20 x 20 m) – x 0.5 the number of NCRN plots

Table A. 1. Percent change in basal area and density of trees ≥ 10 DBH occurring in NCRN plots in 2006. The NCRN plot consists of a 15-m radius circular plot. The square plots are 20 x 20 m in size. Results for square plots are based on the same number as the NCRN or a multiple of that number (indicated in the column header).

	Basal Area				Density			
		Square Plot				Square Plot		
	NCRN	x 1	x 0.75	x 0.50	NCRN	x 1	x 0.75	x 0.50
All Parks	4.9%	5.2%	6.0%	7.3%	5.0%	5.3%	6.1%	7.5%
Manassas NB	17.4%	25.8%	30.1%	37.9%	23.6%	27.0%	31.5%	39.6%
Catoctin MP	14.9%	11.4%	13.3%	16.6%	15.7%	13.9%	16.2%	20.3%
Species	28.8%	28.0%	32.3%	39.7%	24.1%	23.5%	27.2%	33.4%

Figure A. 1. Percent detectable change using different size and number of plots throughout the National Capital Region Network. Analyses are based on trees ≥ 10 cm dbh collected in circular NCRN plots and sub-sampled to smaller square plots (1x, 0.75x, and 0.5x the NCRN plots). α = 0.1.

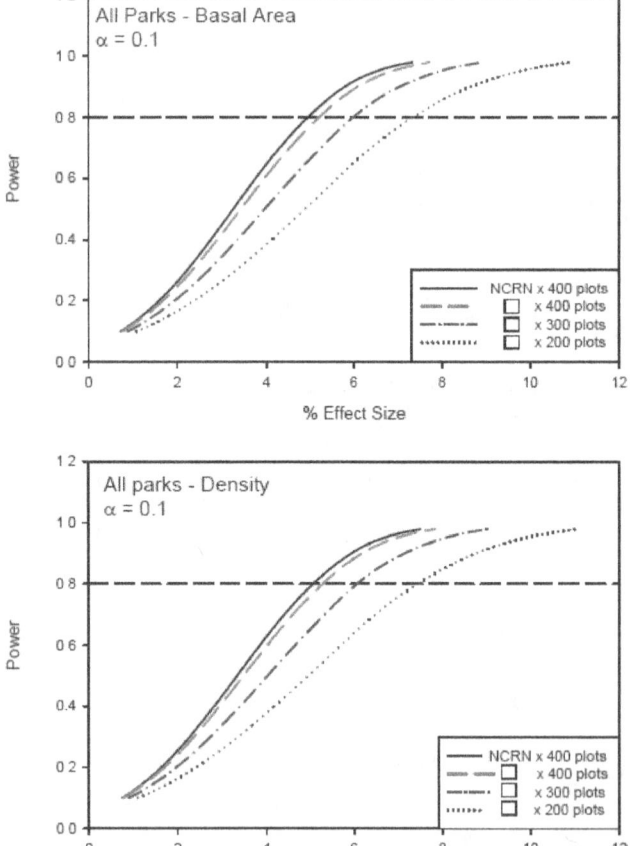

1.4 Results

1.4.1 All parks

The NCRN approach (400 circular plots) had more power than the smaller plots (20 x 20 m plots). The power to detect the same level of change declined as the sample size decreased from 400 to 200 square plots (Figure A. 1). Nevertheless, while the NCRN plots were able to detect a 4.9% change in tree basal area with a power of 0.8, the 300 square plots could detect a 6.0% change at the same power (Table A. 1). Likewise, NCRN plots could detect a 5.0% change in tree density compared to a 6.1% change with 300 square plots.

1.4.2 Manassas NBP

As the total number of plots sampled decreased, the level of change detected with a power of 0.8 declined. We analyzed the results for Manassas NBP (MANA), a park that presents many similarities to the MIDN parks. Six plots were sampled by NCRN in the first year, and our analyses assume the same number of plots would be sampled each year for a total of 24 plots. The analyses for the square plots were conducted based on 24 plots, 18 plots (three-quarters of the total) or 12 plots (half the total). Again, the smaller size and decreasing total number of plots resulted in a decline in the detectable effect size (Figure A. 2). For basal area at a power of 0.8, NCRN plots would detect 17.4% change while 18 square plots would only detect a 30.1% change (Figure A. 2). Likewise, NCRN plots would detect a 23.6% change in tree density while the 18 square plots would detect a 31.5% change.

1.4.3 Catoctin MP

Interestingly, the lower number of smaller plots did not always result in a lower power to detect change, as was observed in Catoctin MP (CATO) (Figure A. 3). Both for basal area and density, the same number of smaller plots were more effective at detecting change than the NCBN plots (basal area change of 11.4% for square versus 14.9% for NCBN at a power of 0.8; density change of 13.9% versus 15.7% respectively) (Figure A. 3). In fact for basal area, 21 square plots had more power than 28 NCRN plots (13.3% versus 14.9%). A closer evaluation of the data revealed that the larger NCRN plots were detecting higher variability than the smaller plots. Though the ecological and cultural setting of CATO is not directly comparable to the MIDN parks, it does illustrate that the variability can vary significantly from one park to the next even at small spatial scales.

1.4.4 Species across network

A similar analysis was conducted to evaluate the power to detect changes in species density and basal area. The same number of NCRN plots and the smaller square plots had similar abilities to detect change at the same power (α = 0.1. Figure A. 4). For basal area, NCRN plots detected a 28.8% change while the smaller plots detected 28.0% (Figure A. 4). For tree density the change detected was 24.1% and 23.5% respectively.

1.4.5 Changes in species density

The power the detect changes in density of individual species was generally low, and decreased with plot size and number (Table A. 2). Only among the most common species such as *Quercus alba*, *Quercus rubra*, *Liriodendron tulipifera*, *Nyssa sylvatica*, *Acer rubrum*, *Fagus grandifolia*, and *Carya tomentosa* were detectable levels below 25% for the NCRN plots.

1.4.6 Loss of species

One area of concern when using smaller plots is what would be missed. In particular, are there any species sampled in the larger NCRN plot that would have been lost if only a 20 x 20 m square plot had been sampled. In fact, this was the case, with five species being lost entirely from the network, including *Amelanchier arborea*, *Amelanchier canadensis*, *Broussonetia papyrifera*, *Ulmus americana*, and *Viburnum prunifolium*. An additional 17 species were lost from individual parks (Table A. 3).

1.5 Discussion

The analyses were conducted with the less conservative α level of 0.1, primarily to increase our power to detect a lower level of change and reduce the size and number of plots needed.

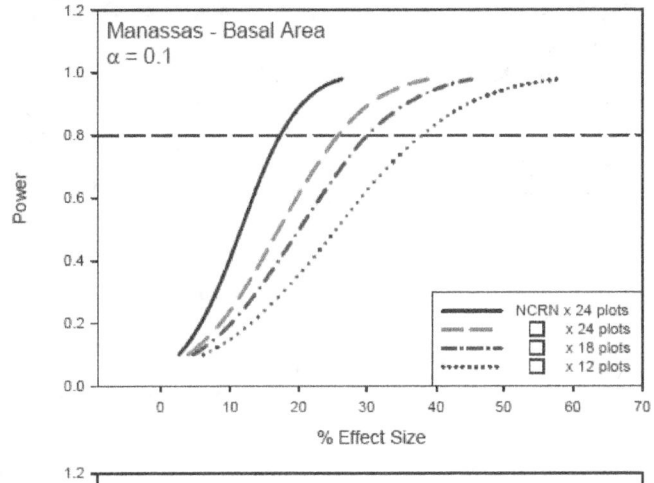

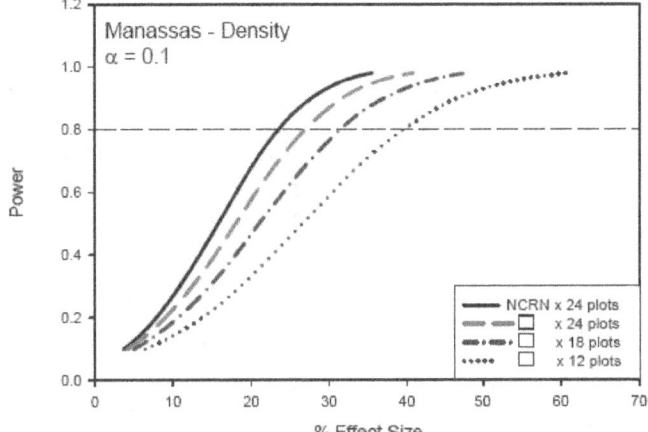

The higher α does increase our chance of detecting a change when none occurred (Type I or false change error), but does err on the side of caution – we are less likely to miss a change when one really did occur. In addition, the analyses were based on spatial variability which is likely to be greater than temporal variability, and therefore the results may be conservative.

In general, the larger NCRN plots detected lower levels of change than the equivalent number of smaller square plots. Decreasing the total number of square plots from 400 to 300 and 200 further decreased their ability to detect change. However, for the same number of plots, the decrease in plot size by 57% accounted for decline in the detectable change in the density and basal area of trees of between 1 and 8%. In fact, in some instances (at CATO) the smaller plots had a greater power to detect change due to lower variability in the data.

Detecting change in the number of individuals of a given species across the network was generally low. Only the most common species provided the ability to detect changes of be-

Figure A. 2. Percent detectable change using different size and number of plots at Manassas National Battlefield Park, VA. Analyses are based on trees ≥ 10 cm dbh collected in circular NCRN plots and sub-sampled to smaller square plots (1x, 0.75x, and 0.5x the NCRN plots). α = 0.1.

Figure A. 3. Percent detectable change using different size and number of plots at Catoctin Mountain Park, MD. Analyses are based on trees ≥ 10 cm dbh collected in circular NCRN plots and sub-sampled to smaller square plots (1x, 0.75x, and 0.5x the NCRN plots). α = 0.1.

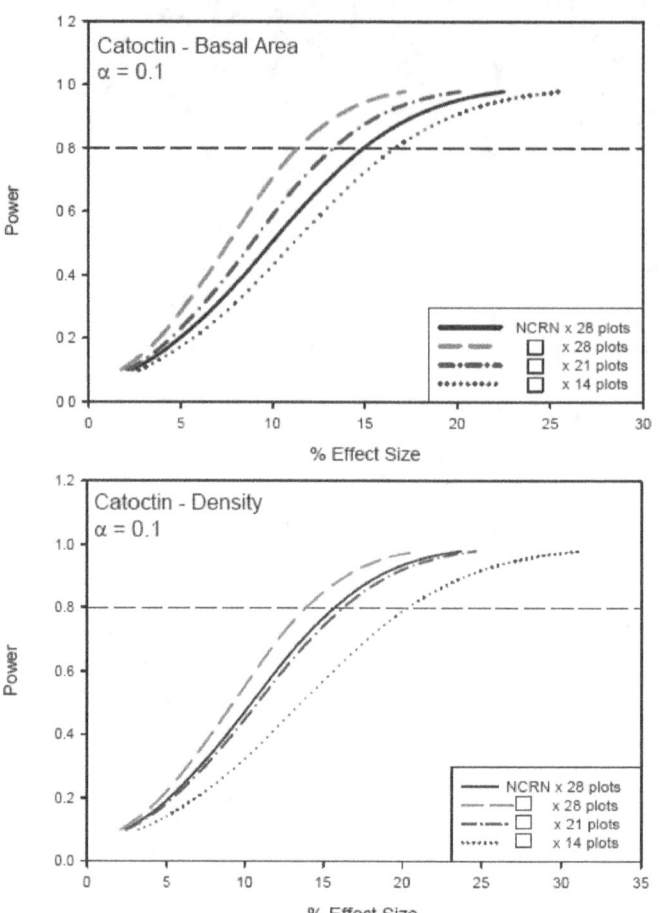

tween 10 and 25% for the NCRN plots. The level detected for smalller and fewer plots was generally higher. Given the small sample sizes, detecting changes in species densities in any given park is unlikely to be possible with a high degree of confidence.

1.6 Conclusion

Based on these results, the MIDN has decided to establish smaller plots, 20 x 20 m plots and to also establish a smaller number across the network (300). Clearly this will reduce the power to detect change, but is based on the networks current staffing and funding level. Once all 300 plots have been established, recensus of these plots will be initiated. At that time it may be possible to increase the number of plots by establishing new ones, and thus increasing the protocols power.

1.7 Literature Cited

Schmit, J. and P. Campbell. 2007. National Capital Region Network 2006 Forest Vegetation Monitoring Report. Natural Resource Report NPS/NCRN/NRTR—2007/046. National Park Service, Fort Collins, Colorado.

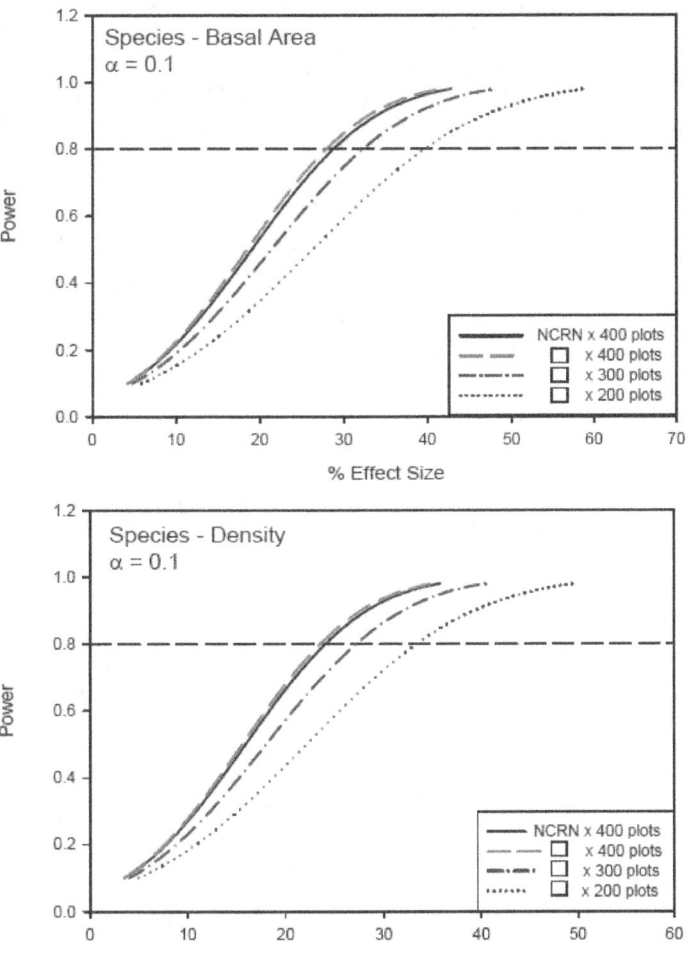

Figure A. 4. Percent detectable change using different size and number of plots in the National Capital Region Network. Analyses are based on trees ≥ 10 cm dbh collected in circular NCRN plots and sub-sampled to smaller square plots (1x, 0.75x, and 0.5x the NCRN plots). α = 0.1.

Table A. 2. Percent change in density for species occurring in NCRN plots in 2006. The NCRN plot consists of a 15-m radius circular plot. The square plots are 20 x 20 m in size. Results for square plots are based on the same number as the NCRN or a multiple of that number.

Species	NCRN	Square Plot		
		x1	x 0.75	x 0.50
Acer negundo	36.7%	35.7%	41.2%	50.6%
Acer rubrum	21.4%	24.2%	27.9%	34.2%
Acer saccharinum	50.2%	57.8%	66.8%	81.9%
Acer saccharum	73.8%	69.6%	80.5%	98.7%
Ailanthus altissima	47.0%	45.6%	52.7%	64.6%
Carya glabra	30.2%	28.7%	33.2%	40.7%
Carya tomentosa	22.2%	25.5%	29.4%	36.1%
Celtis occidentalis	45.1%	47.2%	54.6%	66.9%
Cornus florida	50.6%	71.2%	82.2%	100.9%
Fagus grandifolia	23.7%	24.3%	28.1%	34.5%
Fraxinus americana	41.1%	37.4%	43.2%	52.9%
Fraxinus pennsylvanica	43.1%	47.7%	55.2%	67.7%
Ilex opaca	29.5%	31.8%	36.8%	45.1%
Juglans nigra	43.7%	52.1%	60.2%	73.9%
Juniperus virginiana	53.2%	50.6%	58.5%	71.7%
Liquidambar styraciflua	45.1%	46.5%	53.8%	65.9%
Liriodendron tulipifera	17.7%	19.1%	22.1%	27.1%
Nyssa sylvatica	19.3%	22.0%	25.4%	31.1%
Pinus taeda	71.2%	87.6%	101.2%	124.2%
Pinus virginiana	32.3%	31.3%	36.1%	44.3%
Prunus serotina	47.3%	48.6%	56.2%	68.9%
Quercus alba	19.5%	22.6%	26.1%	32.0%
Quercus coccinea	29.2%	28.5%	32.9%	40.4%
Quercus montana	36.7%	37.6%	43.4%	53.2%
Quercus rubra	24.5%	25.3%	29.2%	35.8%
Quercus stellata	50.0%	61.3%	70.9%	86.9%
Ulmus rubra	32.5%	33.8%	39.1%	48.0%

Table A. 3. Species lost from study or individual parks when a smaller plot is used. Columns show parks[1] where species are lost, with the total number of plots sampled in parentheses.

Species lost from Study	ANTI (1)	CATO (7)	CHOH (23)	GWMP (6)	HAFE (7)	MANA (6)	MONO (6)	NACE (9)	PRWI (35)	ROCR (3)	WOTR (1)
Amelanchier arborea			x								
Amelanchier canadensis				x							
Broussonetia papyrifera					x						
Ulmus americana										x	
Viburnum prunifolium						x					

Species lost from park	ANTI (1)	CATO (7)	CHOH (23)	GWMP (6)	HAFE (7)	MANA (6)	MONO (6)	NACE (9)	PRWI (35)	ROCR (3)	WOTR (1)
Acer saccharinum								x			
Acer saccharum								/	x		
Ailanthus altissima							x				
Amelanchier laevis										x	
Betula lenta			x								
Cercis canadensis					x						
Cornus florida										x	
Fagus grandifolia					x						
Fraxinus pennsylvanica				x							
Pinus virginiana					x						
Platanus occidentalis					x						
Platanus occidentalis						x					
Quercus alba								x			
Quercus palustris					x						
Quercus stellata					x				x		
Tilia americana			x		x						
Ulmus rubra				x							

[1] Parks sampled:

ANTI	Antietam National Battlefield
CATO	Catoctin Mountain Park
CHOH	Chesapeake & Ohio Canal National Historical Park
GWMP	George Washington Memorial Parkway
HAFE	Harpers Ferry National Historical Park
MANA	Manassas National Battlefield Park
MONO	Monocacy National Battlefield
NACE	National Capital Parks-East
PRWI	Prince William Forest Park
ROCR	Rock Creek Park
WOTR	Wolf Trap National Park for the Performing Arts

NPS 956/100130, July 2009